Other Books by Katherine Hetzel

StarMark
Kingstone

The Chronicles of Issraya

Book 1: Tilda of Merjan
Book 2: Tilda and the Mines of Pergatt
Book 3: Tilda and the Bones of Kradlock

Squidge's Guide *to* Super Stories

Squidge's Guide to SUPER STORIES

& BECOMING A BETTER WRITER

Katherine Hetzel

Dragonfeather Books
Bedazzled Ink Publishing Company • Fairfield, California

978-1-949290-68-4 paperback

Cover and interior art
by
Katherine Hetzel

Cover Design
by

Dragonfeather Books
a division of
Bedazzled Ink Publishing, LLC
Fairfield, California
http://www.bedazzledink.com

For every writer, beta-reader, and editor
who has ever helped me with my writing.

Punctuation and terminology disclaimer. The punctuation and terminology used in this book is according to UK conventions, but notes alternatives in certain places.

An Introduction

Everyone is a storyteller. Really. They are.

Think about it. We tell stories whenever we describe what we did at the weekend. What our favourite present was on our last birthday. Where we went on holiday last year ... These are stories about ourselves and our lives, and are more often than not, real.

Not everyone uses words to tell their stories though—some people draw pictures to tell a story. Others take photos. They might dance, or sing, or make a film, or act, or sculpt, or paint ... But there's still a story in there, somewhere.

Bet you could tell one, right now. Imagine you are late for school. Have a think about why—don't spend too long on it and be as wacky as you like. Now go and find someone prepared to listen to your explanation! Or write it down in a 'Dear Teacher, John was late to school today because ...' letter.

What happened, by the way?

Rush into a burning building to save someone?
AWESOME

Did you fall through a portal into another dimension?

Got kidnapped by aliens?
AMAZING!

COOL

See? It's that easy to tell a story.

But it's not always easy to *write* one, and that's why this book exists—chances are, you're reading it because you're already writing stories of your own (or want to begin) and you'd like to know how to make them better. I'm hoping what's inside these pages will help you to capture your story ideas, fill them out, and then polish them up to be the best you can possibly make them.

Why Squidge?

Some of you might be wondering why this book is called *Squidge's* Guide to Super Stories, instead of Katherine's Guide to Super Stories. The short answer is because Squidge is a nickname.

But if you want the long answer, here's the story of how I got the nickname, and why I've used it . . .

I was involved in the Guide Association for many years. On my first camp as a Young Leader, aged just sixteen, all the leaders and Patrols had names to fit a woodland theme. My camp name was Squirrel.

Within half an hour of arriving at the campsite, thanks to the Guides, it had morphed into Squidge—and stayed that way for twenty years.

Although I left the Guide Association, I kept the nickname, and used it as my moniker when I first joined an online writing group. Why did I hide behind a nickname? Well, mainly because I wasn't sure I was a good enough writer to join—if I was rubbish, I didn't want to own up to it. However, once I'd been reassured that the group was a place where I could learn and improve, and that I wasn't as bad as I thought, Squidge became my writing name. I started a blog—Squidge's Scribbles—and in writing about my writing and my life, my family became Mr Squidge and the two Squidgelings.

Being Squidge is such a big part of who I am, I decided to use it in the title of the book—and being a writer, how could I resist a bit of alliteration as well?

BEFORE WE BEGIN . . .

I need to say up front, that I'm *not* a teacher. And when I went to school, they didn't teach the rules of grammar like they do now. I knew a sentence started with a capital letter and ended with a full stop, and I knew what verbs, nouns, and adjectives were. I knew how dialogue should be written and when to start a new paragraph, but that's about it as far as I was taught. Most of what I demonstrate in my writing nowadays, I've learnt through experience—and I've learned a lot.

What I *am*, is a writer, with two collections of short stories and several fantasy novels for children, plus many short stories for adults, already published. And it's my knowledge of story writing that I'm sharing with you.

This book is *not* going to tell you your story has to be perfect when it's finished. In fact, I tell children on school visits that I don't mind if their spelling is awful, or if they forget some of their capital letters and full stops—I'm more interested in capturing a story first and thinking about the rules after. They look at me as if I'm mad. They can't believe they're allowed to write a story without paying attention to things like that. But what I've found is that often, when you take away the so-called 'rules' of writing—at least to begin with—you stop worrying about how perfect your writing needs to be and end up creating some really amazing stories.

Yes, you will need to polish your writing and I'll help you with some of that, but for now, I want you to have fun, and not worry about the rules—yet.

Using this book

This book is not intended to be an instruction manual as such. What's in it is the kind of information and advice I share with young and novice writers so that they can look towards improving the stories they have already written, or want to begin writing. You can dip in and out of it to find the areas you need help with, or read through the lot and take it all in . . . As you'll discover as you read on, it's entirely up to you.

You might want to keep a pen and paper handy too, because as you work through the book, you'll find a few exercises to try along the way. They aren't essential for you to do though—I'm not setting homework!

Chapter 1

How to be a better writer

I'm often asked what you need to be a good writer. Is there a magic formula somewhere you can drink? A special pen you can buy that only writes bestsellers? A set of failsafe rules that you can follow?

Sadly, no. But there are some things I've noticed that good and improving writers always do.

1. Writers write

I know, I know, it sounds obvious. But good writers write. And the more they write, the better they get, usually. I mean, you don't get to play an instrument well without practising, do you? You aren't selected for the football team of your dreams if you haven't trained hard, and you probably won't paint a masterpiece the first time you pick up a brush.

Writing takes practice.

So writers write. Some write purely for fun, or because they can't imagine not writing. Some write to please themselves, others because they want to be published. Some of them write every single day. Others write only at the weekend. Some write early in the morning, others late at night. They might set themselves a target to write so many words at a time, or keep writing from dawn to dusk and only stop when they've filled pages and pages in a session. They might write in a proper study, or sitting on their beds, or in a shed at the bottom of the garden. Some will write by hand, and others will type everything on a computer. Some like to listen to music as they write, others prefer silence.

I write in longish sessions, but not every day, often singing along to favourite music. I either sit on one end of the sofa or on the floor in front of it, or squish into a bean bag in my garden room. I use pen and paper for working out ideas, but a laptop for typing them up.

That's what works for me . . .

I can't tell you what is going to work for *you*, though. You'll have to do some experimenting.

What's important to remember is that there's no magic mix of time or place or method that suits everyone exactly the same to get the writing done. What works for you is something you will have to figure out for yourself. And it might change, depending on your circumstances or the mood you're in.

The important thing to do while you *are* figuring it out is that wherever, whenever, and however you choose to write, you keep writing.

2. Writers read

Writers read lots.

When I was younger, I was a bookworm. So much so, that at Christmas, book-shaped presents were always found right at the bottom of the present pile. Father Christmas must've known that if I unwrapped a book early on, I'd not open anything else until I'd finished reading it . . .

I used to go to the town library frequently as a child, and we even had the luxury of a library van that stopped both ends of my street every Friday afternoon. (If I missed the first stop, you can bet I was on the van for the second!) I remember taking my six books out on the Friday before we set off on holiday on the Saturday, and I'd have read *all* of my brother's and sister's books *and* my own by the time we came home, two weeks later.

Mostly, I read fiction, but I also read comics, magazines, and newspapers. As I got older, I branched out, reading autobiographies, biographies, graphic novels, articles on the internet . . . Because, you see, good writers often read *widely*.

If you like reading, read whatever you enjoy reading. If you like books about Ancient Egypt, read them. If you prefer graphic novels, don't be put off by anyone who says they're not proper books or belittles them for being one step up from a comic. The important thing is that you are still reading–heck, even a shopping list is reading. (Though it's not very interesting, normally.) Don't be afraid to try reading new things. As a child, I preferred fantasy and adventure stories, but as I got older I tried reading horror, mysteries, comedy, real-life accounts . . . Some things I don't enjoy–I'm not a fan of detective novels, for example–but at least I tried them. People sometimes tell me they don't like reading, and my reply is always that they've not found the right book yet, and to keep looking.

By reading, you absorb good things. You'll see words you don't know being used–look up what they mean and use them yourself. You'll start to see what *that* author does to make his story-world feel really real, even though you know the Planet Haldant can't possibly exist. Or you'll realise what little tricks *this* author uses to make her ghost story *so* scary. Be like a sponge, and soak it all up!

3. Writers write the story only they can write

If I give a roomful of students the same prompt for a story, I can guarantee that no two stories will be the same. They will be as different as the people who wrote them. And it doesn't matter!

The best compliment I ever had was from a friend who read something I'd written and said, 'that's a Squidge story!' It meant I'd written something only *I* could have written.

Imagine you are given a book with a plain cover, no hint on it of who the author is, or what the title might be. As you read the story, would you be able to recognise your favourite author, purely by the way they write? My favourite author is Terry Pratchett (look him up if you've not heard of him—his Discworld novels are great fun) and I'm sure I'd be able to recognise his work, because he has a distinct style and a way with words that is his, and his only. He has, we would say, a distinct writing voice.

It can take a while until you find *your* voice—that unique way of writing that you have—but until then, keep writing and experimenting and eventually it'll come.

At the end of the day, only *you* can write a story in *your* way.

4. Writers don't give up

"It takes years to achieve an overnight success."

I can't remember who said that, but it's actually true. No-one turns out a bestseller at their first attempt—or at least, it happens very rarely. And how people measure success varies enormously. Not everyone writes to be published, which is often how success in viewed in writing. But if that *is* something you would like to work towards, then you need to keep writing.

It took me about ten years from starting to write seriously until my first book was published. Over that time, I kept writing, learnt an awful lot about writing, and kept improving until *finally* I had something I felt was good enough to become a real book.

Even then, a lot of people didn't like what I'd written. Unfortunately, whatever you write, however good your writing is, there'll always be some people who don't like it. They might want more aliens. Less romance. They don't like your main character's name, or think the story would be better if it ended differently. Sometimes they just don't like the way you've chosen to write it. And it hurts to hear things like that.

> At one point, hearing it hurt me so badly, I gave up writing. I thought I was a rubbish writer, even if I did have loads of exciting stories running round inside my head, begging to be written. It took a year before I picked up my pen and started to write again, but I've never stopped for as long, since.

If the same thing happens to you, you're allowed to feel sad or angry about it. But try not to feel that way for long. Pick up your pen and try again.

You never know, being told these kind of things might fire you up to become more determined than ever. It might motivate you to keep writing until one day you write something that you are really proud of, and who knows *what* might happen after that?

Basically, if you really want to be a writer, if you can't imagine *not* writing, then don't give up. Good writers don't. They carry on, but they develop a thicker skin.

5. Writers save everything

In a time where computers are commonly used, it's very easy to press delete if you don't like what you've written. And in a move to save the planet, we're getting keener to recycle paper—which might include the notebook you've decided to throw out, even though there's a scrappy story in it that you wrote two years ago.

I would urge you to keep everything you write. Make sure to save your work regularly on a computer if you are using one, *and* back it up! Hang onto your notebooks, because, who knows, one day you might be giving a talk about the books you've had published, and you'll be able to show it to a roomful of people and tell them that this messy work turned into *insert title of imaginary book here*, like I do.

If you like doing writing exercises, sometimes they can become part of a bigger story. You get a sudden flash of inspiration, and can see *exactly* how that description you wrote of the man on the bus—the one with the crocodile-headed walking stick and green silk waistcoat—will fit a character in a story. Heck, he might even end up having the whole story written about him!

If you've written something longer—half a story perhaps, or even a whole one—but you're not entirely happy with it, hang onto it. At the very least, as you write more and improve, you'll be able to look back over it and say, "look how much better I am at writing now than I was!"

Old stories can sometimes be resurrected—in whole or in part—as I proved with my third published novel, which I'd worked on for many years until I believed it was good enough. (It had a brand new main character, too!)

So, let's just recap what you'll need to do, to become a good writer.

You need to write (lots). Read (lots). Write *your* way. Don't give up. And save everything.

With all these things in mind, are you ready to have a go at writing and improving your own stories?

Yes? Then let's crack on . . .

Chapter 2

Finding the spark
—Ideas and inspiration

It helps that I've always had a very active imagination and I used to daydream a lot, so I find it relatively easy to come up with ideas for stories. But you don't necessarily need to be imaginative to be inspired. Beautiful writing or good stories don't rely entirely on imagination. They can be based on real things too, as we're about to find out.

NOTICING

"Where do you get your ideas from?" is one of the questions I'm most often asked. And the answer is usually "Everywhere!"

Which isn't very helpful, is it? Even if it's true.

What I *mean* is that ideas come from all around me, because a writer needs to *notice*. It might be something you hear, or see, or experience, and a lightbulb goes off in your head.

You think things like 'Oooh, a see-through guitar. What if it was made of crystal? Who'd play that?' Or you see a table with tiger feet carved into the bottom of its legs, and you imagine what would happen if the table walked away.

Sometimes what you notice doesn't give you the idea for a whole story, but becomes a detail in a room, or the way a character might behave. All *you* have to do is notice it . . .

Ideas are tricky little things though; they are very good at slipping away. That's why I always suggest that you catch them somehow.

You could take a photograph of an unusual building; draw the funny hat the lady on the bus was wearing; have a treasure box for quirky or interesting little objects. Simplest of all, you can write about The Thing you've noticed.

I normally write or draw what I've noticed in a notebook. In lots of notebooks, actually, because I always have a small one with me when I'm out and about, another by my bed in case of lying-awake-at-midnight inspiration or things I remember from weird dreams . . . and one in the lounge, where I do most of my writing.

I'm a *very* vivid dreamer, often dreaming in colour and able to feel things, too. If I want a wild or wacky story, I just have to read through one of my dreams!

Now assuming you've noticed something, caught it, and kept it, you might not use it straightaway. I've never written *The Crystal Guitar,* but it's still in my notebook, waiting. (Remember I said good writers never throw anything anyway ...?) Some people are really good at noticing things and using them in their stories. But what if you aren't very good at noticing yet? What if you need a bit more help to get you started on a story?

PROMPTS

I think I'm pretty good at using things I've noticed to spark a story idea, but when I get stuck—which does still happen sometimes—I use a writing prompt. This is basically an idea that someone else has come up with to kickstart *their* writing, which might be good to get my brain sparking with ideas, too.

Here are some I've used before. Why not have a go at one or two—or all—of them, yourself?

Three things

On school visits I often take a Story Bag with me. Students pull three things out of it and write a story that includes all of them. Here's a sample bag:

a coin
a tin of baked beans
a toy police car
a rainbow-striped sock
a 'crystal' necklace
a dragon

an elephant
a wooden spoon
a rusty key
a heart-shaped stone
a small candle

Choose three things from the list and write a story that includes them all. If you want the full Story Bag experience, write each item on separate slips of paper and pull three out of a sock. Not the rainbow one though.

Seven
by seven
by seven

It feels a bit like cheating, but you can use someone else's writing as a prompt.

If you have a bookshelf, pick up the seventh book on it. Turn to the seventh page. What's the first complete sentence that starts on the seventh line? Use it as the opening sentence or basis of a story.

Doors

Choose one of these doors. Decide what's behind it. Now write about what happens when you open it . . .

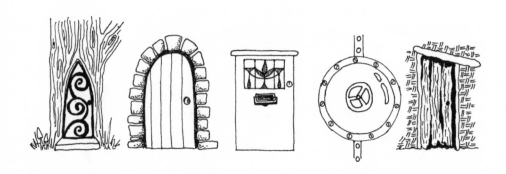

I remember . . .

Think about an event, like a favourite holiday. A memorable Christmas. Last Halloween. Your first day at school. Give yourself ten minutes and write down everything you remember about it—but every sentence must begin with 'I remember . . .'

Write a story now about that day or event, and include some of what you remembered.

Take one title

Here are some imaginary titles. Choose one and write the story to go with it.

The Mystery of the Missing Mouse
Crocodile Style
The Dream Weaver
The Cloak of Mystery
The Library Guard
The Dancer and the Dragon
Demon's Curse
The Last Star
Benjamin's Buttons

Opening lines

As the name suggests, you have a sentence or two that would make a good opening for a story.

"One last time," he whispered.

The Keeper of the Keys had been summoned early to the palace.

I saved your kingdom from destruction. I have come to claim my reward.

Everyone thought I'd forget. But I remembered everything.

It was the colour that attracted his attention first.

The timer was down to the last thirty seconds.

Headlines

When you read a headline, do you ever wonder about the story behind it before you read it? Here are a few real headlines:

POLICE SOLVE CASE OF MISSING BACON

THERE GOES CHRISTMAS

ESCAPED KING COBRA VISITS GYM

TEACHER BREAKS 'SWUGGLING' RECORD

The mind boggles . . . but pick one and write your version of what happened.

You can also write your own headlines. Insert a number [#] or a word where indicated into the headline, then write the article.

[#] best [tricks/tips] to boost [something] (e.g. 101 Best Tricks to Boost Your Snargalump's Appetite)

[#] reasons why your [something] is not [doing what it's supposed to] (e.g. Three Reasons Why Your Snargalump's Not Behaving)

[# Topic] and how to avoid them (e.g. Thirteen Snargalump Diseases and How to Avoid Them)

[Something] made simple (e.g. Knitting Snargalump Socks Made Simple)

Finding **prompts** for yourself

The internet is an amazing place, full of potential prompts. But do be careful what you use as a search term, because you may get some very peculiar results or discover more than you bargained for . . .

I use the internet a lot for picture prompts on a theme—anything from 'unusual vehicles' to 'interesting faces' or 'imaginary places'.

Generators—computer-based, random word machines—are a good source of inspiration too. Some will give you three words to use—a bit like the three objects prompt. Others might give you titles to suit a particular genre or theme, though sometimes what they come up with can be a bit bonkers and won't make much sense! When that happens to me, I cheat. I click 'new title' and keep doing that until I come across something that takes my fancy. And there are name generators too . . .

Simply searching 'writing prompts for children/adults' will take you to a huge number of writing sites, writers' blogs, educational sites . . . You can even buy books, filled with nothing but writing prompts.

As I said before, *anything* can become a prompt. I've used paint charts, LEGO minifigures, gravestone inscriptions, song titles . . . Keep a record of them all, and one day, you might be able to help someone else spark off from a prompt which *you* discovered.

" "

My son loved LEGO, and as a result, he collected lots of their little minifigures. If you're the same, find out your minifigures because they can give you a character either as they are—*or when you mix and match bits of them!* Chop and change legs and bodies and accessories, see what kind of interesting people you can come up with. A story about a Stetson-wearing spaceman, anyone?

"

Chapter 3

Getting going —
the Writing Process

Once you have your inspiration, saying to yourself 'I'm going to write a story about that' is really exciting.

Then you turn on your computer and fire up a blank screen, or pull a clean sheet of paper towards you and pick up your pen, and writing a story seems suddenly so . . . BIG!

You stare at that screen or sheet of paper, knowing that you want to get your ideas into sort some of shape that looks and reads like a real story, but how do you begin?

Well, for starters, how do you like to work when you are writing?

Planner—
or Pantser?

Assuming you've got an idea you want to work with, do you, a) plan everything out in detail first? Or b) just get going, and see where the story takes you?

Neither way is wrong—and neither is right, either. When people work creatively, some like to plan everything before they start, while others don't care for planning.

For example, imagine two painters . . .

One might know exactly what he wants his finished picture to look like before he even starts. He'll have made a few pencil sketches, gathers all his brushes and paints together. He might even mix *exactly* the right shade of blue for the sky before he puts any paint on the canvas.

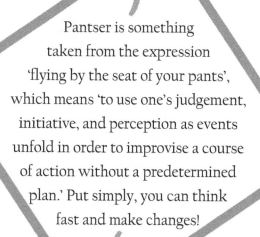

HE'S A PLANNER.

Pantser is something taken from the expression 'flying by the seat of your pants', which means 'to use one's judgement, initiative, and perception as events unfold in order to improvise a course of action without a predetermined plan.' Put simply, you can think fast and make changes!

The other might just grab whatever colour takes her fancy, slap the paint on, and see where the mood takes her until she feels she's finished.

SHE'S A PANTSER.

It's the same with writing. Some writers like to plan; they use sticky notes or character files (you'll learn about these later) or diagrams to show how all the different bits of the story fit together, all before they even write a single sentence. Others will take their spark of an idea, start writing about it immediately, and see what springs to mind along the way.

I am more of a Plantser—I do a little bit of both. I've tried detailed planning, but my own creative mind seems to work best if I don't try to pin the story down too much. At the start of a story I usually know who my main character will be and what will have happened to them by the time I get to the end, but how I get them from the start to the end is often a bit of a mystery. Once I start writing, I have lots of fun finding out, though!

You might already know if you are a Planner, a Pantser, or a Plantser. If you don't, there's no harm in trying different ways of working creatively. Eventually, you will find something that feels right and comfortable for you, even if it's nothing like the way anyone else works.

♫ I did it myyyy waaayyyy! ♫

If you enjoy reading (and I hope you do—remember it will help your writing) you will probably have realised that no two authors write alike. I don't mean that one writes adventures, another ghost stories, another one fantasy. I'm talking about what we refer to in the writing world the author's voice. I don't mean their speaking voice, I mean their writing one. The way they use the words they've chosen, and how they string them together.

I have quite a chatty, informal style (which you'll probably have noticed by now!), and I use a lot of dialogue and action in my stories, but don't tend to write long descriptive passages. That's not to say I don't write any description at all, but when I do, I keep it to a minimum and fairly simple. If I were to compare my own writing to that of other authors, I could easily think that perhaps my descriptions need to be longer and more detailed, or that I should be using more complicated vocabulary. I might even think that I should be writing more like them . . .

The problem with thinking like that is that you become unsatisfied with the way *you* write. I spent quite a few years trying to write the way other authors wrote, before finally discovering that my own stories were much better when I kept things simple. I reached a point where I could tell myself,

"Write what you CAN, not what you CAN'T."

This mantra doesn't stop me admiring how other authors write and it doesn't keep me from trying to write in ways that don't come naturally to me occasionally. But it *does* remind me to write to my strengths, and in my own voice.

The more you write your own stories, the more you will discover what your strengths are and what your voice is like. And when you do—wow! That's writing as only *you* can write it.

What kind of story to write—
Genre

You can write a story about ANYTHING! It's *your* story and you can write whatever you want to. You could write a story about an orange dragon who eats nothing but baked beans—which means she fires flames out of her bottom! Or you could write one about a boy who's lost his memory and is trying to find out where he really came from. If it's a story you want to tell, go for it!

You might find that to begin with, you write the kind of stories you like to read the most. For me, that's Fantasy. For you, it might be any one or more of the following:

I could probably think of a few more, but you get my drift. All of them are different genres—groups of similar types of stories.

It's generally a good idea to know roughly what genre you're aiming for before you start, although sometimes a story might be a combination of different genres. Like a space-themed whodunnit for example. Or a historical love story perhaps, or a fantasy adventure.

Starting off writing in one genre doesn't mean you have to stick to the same thing all the time. I started out writing fantasy and it's still my preferred genre, but over time I experimented with others. I don't think I'll ever be a crime writer because I don't enjoy reading thrillers and I'm not very good at holding all the twists and turns that keep a reader guessing "Who did it?" But I have dabbled with ghost stories, horror, comedy, sci-fi, and romance so far.

Don't be afraid to experiment with writing something you're not used to writing, or that you've always wanted to have a go at. You never know, you might find out that you're brilliant at it.

Equally, though, if you find you're good at writing in one particular genre and don't want to write anything else, it is perfectly fine to stick with it.

Like so many things in the writing world, only you can decide what you are going to write about.

Write what you know, or find out about it—
Research

There is a 'rule' of writing (it's not a rule really—more of a suggestion) that you should only write what you know.

Just take a moment to think about that. How many of your favourite stories would not exist if that rule had been obeyed? Did C.S. Lewis go to Narnia himself before he could write about it? Is J.K. Rowling a witch? Was Jeff Kinney the Wimpy Kid when he was younger?

Of course not.

On the other hand . . .

If you're a brilliant tennis player, and you're writing a story that includes tennis-playing characters, fab. If you're a survival expert and are writing about a shipwrecked sailor, brilliant. If you like collecting stamps, and you're writing about the most expensive stamp in the world getting stolen, amazing!

It means that you can add details to your story that only a tennis player/survival expert/stamp boffin would know, which all helps to make the story more believable to readers who *don't* know any of that stuff. On that basis, I could write about people who knit socks or work in a laboratory, but I'm not sure a story about a sock-knitting scientist would be very interesting!

If *I* wanted to write a survival story, I'd have to do some research first. Research is great. You can find out so many new things! In writing my novels, I've learned about the language of heraldic shields; how to make a slingshot from string; how to melt precious metals; what old mines were like; what the different parts of a ship are called. Not all of these went into the same story of course! In fact, why don't you pick one of those now, and see what you can find out about it for yourself? Do an internet search, watch a video, look it up in the library . . .

When I showed an early draft of this book to a writing friend, he said, "Are you kidding? She could be smuggling out new medicines in the socks she knits at work!" So maybe that story's not so boring as I thought . . .

The problem with research is that when you've discovered all these lovely new facts, you might want to put them *all* into your story because they are so interesting!

DON'T

If you include *everything*, it can sound like you're trying to teach your reader something, rather than letting them enjoy a story. I find it best to sprinkle in enough facts to make it sound like I know what I'm talking about and make the story sound believable.

By all means, do some research if you have to. But make sure what you write doesn't end up sounding more like an instruction manual than a story.

Unless, of course, your character *needs* some detailed instructions on exactly how to smuggle miraculous medicines out of a top secret laboratory in their hand-knitted socks . . .

Chapter 4
Working the Story Out—
Plotting

When we talk about plotting, we're actually talking about how we as writers arrange the sequence of events to carry a reader through the story from beginning to end. Before we get into more detail, let's look at some general story types or outlines.

STORY TYPES

If we took a hundred different books from all sorts of different genres and studied the outlines of their stories, we'd probably find that all of them will fall into one of several *story types*.

Many people have studied story types in much more detail than me. For this book, I'm going to focus on the seven I see most commonly used by young and novice writers. Here's a brief description of each of them.

Overcoming the Monster. The main character in your story finds out about a great evil and sets out to destroy it. This might be a literal monster, or it could be—for example—a spy trying to defeat a plan to overthrow a government.

Rags to Riches. The main character starts off down on their luck, but eventually his/her luck changes and they get their happy ever after.

The Quest. The main character has something that they desperately want/need to find, and sets off to find it, often with friends or helpers.

Voyage and Return. The main character sets off to an unfamiliar place, has adventures while they are there, and comes home a changed person.

Comedy. We tend to think of comedy as something funny, but in this instance, the storyline is more about mix-ups and misunderstandings. The hero and heroine are destined to be together, but other people and events stand in their way, resulting in confusion until something happens that clears up all the misunderstandings and they get their happy ever after.

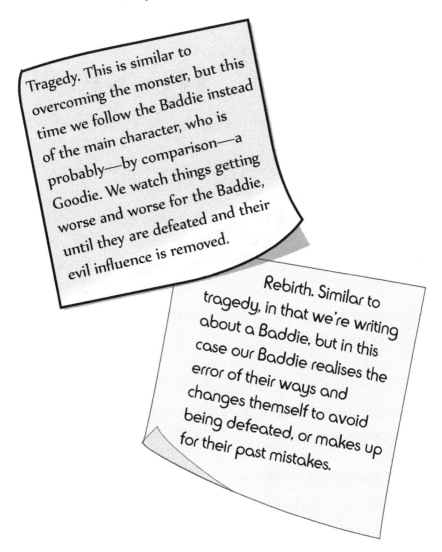

Tragedy. This is similar to overcoming the monster, but this time we follow the Baddie instead of the main character, who is probably—by comparison—a Goodie. We watch things getting worse and worse for the Baddie, until they are defeated and their evil influence is removed.

Rebirth. Similar to tragedy, in that we're writing about a Baddie, but in this case our Baddie realises the error of their ways and changes themself to avoid being defeated, or makes up for their past mistakes.

These outlines sound reasonably simple, and you are probably reading them and thinking that stories are far more complicated. You're right. Think of these types as overviews—a big picture view—of a story from beginning to end. What you're going to do is take one of them and add the complicated stuff to turn it into a proper story.

ALL STORIES
ARE THE SAME . . .

HONEST

There are millions of stories in the world, and every one is different.

Well, they are, but when you look closely, the core of every story is very similar.

That's because a story is usually based around a character. The character has a problem. They have to try different things to solve the problem. The problem is solved and as a result, the character is changed. Now that's a plot at its very simplest, (often called the Hero Journey) and from these basics you can grow your story.

Two of my books are about a character called Granny Rainbow. She's very good at helping other people to solve their problems. And she does it the same way every time.

❶ She meets someone with a problem.

❷ She makes up one of her special magical and colourful potions or powders.

❸ The person with the problem uses the potion or powder.

❹ The problem is solved.

In one story, she helps a violinist win a talent competition. In another, she patches up a friendship that turns sour. She even helps a circus master to put the stripes back onto his circus tent . . .

Stop for a minute and think about some of your favourite books. Identify the main character, the *main* problem they face (there will probably be more than one to overcome in longer stories), and how the problem is solved.

THE STRUCTURE OF A STORY

We've said that all stories are the same, though some might be more complicated than others. There's something else that's the same too.

Every story has a beginning, a middle, and an end.

THE BEGINNING

This is where we are introduced to the main character and the world they live in—it sets the scene for what comes after. It often includes The Thing (the problem we've mentioned) that sets your character off on their adventure, whether that's to find love, kill the dragon, deliver the secret package, find their way home, or stop the wicked wizard.

THE MIDDLE

This is where most of the action happens, and problems get put in the character's way as they try to achieve their goal until—at the climax, not the end—you've got the reader sitting on the edge of their seat because things are looking so bad for your character, the reader can't see how they will ever succeed.

THE END

This is where often, the characters succeed in what they set out to do. Not always—stories don't always have to have a happy ending. This section offers the resolution, or way that the problem is solved, and the story finishes in a satisfactory way, whether that's a good way or a sad way. (I prefer a happy ending to a sad one myself, whether I'm writing or reading, but not everyone does.) Sometimes the ending leaves you hanging, wondering what happens next. This may be deliberate if the story is part of a series.

But let's assume for the purposes of you learning about writing that you're going to be working on one standalone (not part of a series) story.

WHAT'S IN THE BOTTLE?

This is a really simple prompt that can help you to come up with ideas for a story, and then put them in an order that gives you a basic plot. Let's work through it and see how we get on.

To begin with, we're *not* going to write the story. We're going to capture your ideas and recognise where in the story they fit by working through some steps.

Here goes . . .

STEP 1   Choose one of the three bottles, doesn't matter which. If none of them appeal to you, find yourself a picture of one that does. I have a selection of photos of different bottles, and have used them to tell lots of different stories.

STEP 2   Ask yourself 'what's in the bottle?' and list all the things you can think of. Take no longer than a few minutes to do this. There's no right answer, and you can be as weird and wacky as you like.

> When I've done this in the past with writers of all ages, the bottles have contained superpowers, miniature worlds, poison, love potion, unicorn tears, the ghost of a sailor, seven scales from the tail of a mermaid, goblin snot (my personal favourite), and many other things.

STEP 3   Now pick one thing from your list, and describe how it got into the bottle. (If you're up for a bit more of a challenge, include who put it in there as well.)

STEP 4   Someone wants what's in the bottle. Who? Describe them. Why do they want it?

STEP 5   What happens when they get it?

STEP 6 By combining steps 3, 4, and 5, write an outline of events that will become your story. At this point, you may well find yourself asking other questions to help you fill it out. (Who, What, Why, How, When?) That's fine—do as much as you need to, to get that story outline to a point where you are happy with it.

This next section is me, working through these steps for myself:

Which bottle? The long necked one.

What's in it? Crocodile tears, moonlight, powdered unicorn horn, mermaid tears, the seed of a rare plant, melted snow.

Pick one . . . The seed of a money tree, put into the bottle by a famous botanist, Dr Herbert Crinklecut.

Who wants it and why? Lord Biltington-Bother wants the seed because although he seems rich, he's spent all his money on goldfish.

What happens? He grows the tree but it doesn't grow money, it grows monkeys!

Outline the story: Lord B-B steals the bottle because he wants to grow a money tree so he doesn't have to sell all his goldfish. What he doesn't know is Dr C wrote the label on the bottle wrong—it should have read 'monkey tree'. Lord

B-B grows the tree in his garden and ends up with lots of monkeys. This makes him even more desperate for money. But then he has the idea of setting up a zoo and an aquarium, and charging people to visit them. They buy enough tickets to keep the monkeys in nuts, and Lord B-B can keep all his goldfish.

Now if you've worked through the steps for yourself, you may well have realised that what came out of the last step is your plot.

So now, write your story, based on your plot.

Take all the time you need . . .

FINDING THE **RIGHT** TITLE

If you *are* having a go at writing the bottle story, then you might have also come up with a title for it.

Strictly speaking, a title isn't necessary when you're working your ideas into something more concrete, but some authors find it helpful to have one from the very start of the story writing process.

For example, if my bottle had contained the record of the bad things done by a character called Senna, I might have in my head from the very start of planning an outline a title like 'The Seven Sins of Senna', or 'Senna's Sins'. It captures the essence of the story and will hopefully give any future readers an idea of what to expect when they read the finished story.

It's great if you can find a title straight away, but don't worry if you can't. I rarely have a title in my head from the very beginning. I tend to give each story a working title–something that will do until I can work out what the title should be. In my *Chronicles of Issraya* series, the working titles were Tilda #1, Tilda #2, all the way through to Tilda #5. The first three became *Tilda of Merjan*, *Tilda and the Mines of Pergatt*, and *Tilda and the Bones of Kradlock*. I still have to find suitable titles for Tildas 4 and 5!

Sometimes you won't even know what the title's going to be until you've written the whole story. One short story I wrote for adults was a bit of a murder mystery, and it wasn't until I'd got right to the end of it and the murder had been committed that I realised the whole story centred around an object which linked past and present, as well as various characters. It became *The Pink Feather Boa Incident* as a result.

Titles can be a struggle to find, and sometimes you've just got to play with words and ideas until something clicks and you find what sounds right for your story (or book). By the way—there's no copyright (ownership) of titles, so there's nothing at all to stop you from giving your story the same title as another one.

Make sure the title reflects something of what your story is about without giving too much away. No good calling it *Fred the Wizard* if the story is all about Fred finding out that that's what he is.

THE STORY MOUNTAIN

Right, have you had a go at writing the bottle story? How did it go? Hopefully you didn't find it too difficult, and you've got something that looks and feels like a story, even if it's not perfect. At the very least you should be able to see which bits make up the beginning, the middle, and the end of it.

You might be looking at your story and thinking 'it's really simple'. We could add extra interest to the characters and places you've chosen, but first, let's get the plot sorted. Can we make it even more interesting than what we've already got?

Let me introduce you to the idea of the Story Mountain.

Have you ever actually climbed a mountain? I have!

You start off in the valley where there's lots of grass or maybe fields, and you begin to climb. Slowly, the ground gets steeper and rougher. There may not be many trees or bushes, just tough grass and sheep tracks. The path may have to go down instead of up in some places, but all the while you're climbing higher. After hours, you start to think *surely* this has to be the top of the mountain. But when you get there, there's *another* steeper and rockier bit that was hidden from view and you've got even *more* mountain to climb before you reach the real summit. Eventually though, you get to the top and you look at the amazing view (unless you're in fog. I climbed a mountain once and all I could see at the top was whiteness) and you're so pleased with yourself! All that effort was worth it. And then you begin the descent, which is often easier and quicker than the climb up.

That's the kind of experience you're going to give your character(s) in your story. Not a literal mountain climb, though climbing a mountain can make for a good story.

We're going to expand our simple beginning, middle, and end into something more complicated and add more plot *within* each of those sections.

A picture might help . . .

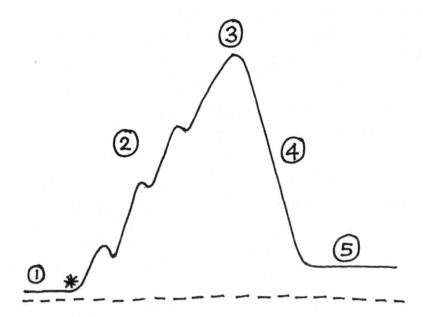

This is the valley, the beginning, where we introduce the characters and setting. Note the asterisk: * is The Problem—the event that changes everything for your main character(s) and makes them react.

❶

BACKGROUND

❷

RISING ACTION

All the events that happen *before* the worst thing ever. There are mini-peaks here, because each event might be a new problem that the character has to overcome before they can move forward in the story. The problems can be caused by the character themself, (they turned left when they should've turned right) or by other people or situations they have no control over (someone switched the road signs), but gradually things get worse and worse until the reader wonders how the character is ever going to succeed.

❸ CLIMAX

This is where the worst possible thing that *could* happen, does! And there's no obvious way to solve it. Everything looks terrible. But not for long . . .

This is where the character(s) work to solve the problem or conflict. It's a steep part of the mountain, because it's often the most action-packed bit of the story, where a few actions have *big* consequences.

❹ FALLING ACTION

❺ RESOLUTION

How things end up—hopefully a lot calmer. Notice it's not at the same level as the valley, where we started the journey. That's because by the end of the story, *something* has to have changed. It could be to do with the character or the world they live in, but there *will* be a change—for better or worse.

Take a look at your bottle story again. Can you see it as a mountain now? Did you make your character(s) work really hard to get up to the top by putting more than one problem in their way, or was it more of a gentle stroll up a hill with only one thing they had to do to resolve their problem? Whichever you chose is absolutely fine.

Going back to Lord B-B . . . The Problem is that he runs out of money. The rising action covers whatever he does to get hold of the bottle with the seed and growing it, and may well include what goes wrong in trying to do that. The climax will be the moment he discovers that it's not a money tree but a *monkey* tree. He's now got no money, and he's got monkeys to look after as well as his fish. His decision to build the zoo and aquarium starts the falling action, and the resolution is the point where he opens both and starts selling tickets.

Remember though, whether you are using the story mountain idea *or* working just on a beginning, middle, end approach, treat them as tools to help you, rather than rules that have to be obeyed.

This is only one of many different ways you can use to plan out a plot. I use it because it's a familiar method found in schools, and simple enough for many beginners to understand. I'm not going to cover any other methods, but if you are interested in looking at other ways, research things like the 3-Act Structure, or Snowflake Method, or Mind Mapping. You may find a way that you understand and like working with more than the Story Mountain, or you might end up picking and choosing little bits from different methods. Like I've said before—try them and see what suits you and your creative self.

KEEPING THE STORY MOVING—PACE

Have you ever read a book and started flicking through pages because nothing seems to be happening? I have. Equally, have you ever read a book and ended up feeling exhausted because the story is full of action that never lets up? Done that, too.

If we go back to the mountain analogy, it's the difference between a long, slow, slog to the top with your granny, or trying to keep pace with your super-fit uncle who runs up and down hills for fun.

What might be a better approach would be to take the tough bits of the climb slowly, and speed up a little when the going gets easier. In other words, you adapt your pace to the terrain.

In the same way, you pace your story. It will speed up and slow down.

Knowing exactly where to speed up or slow down is something that only the writer can decide, but the overall aim is to keep the reader moving all the time through the story without boring or exhausting them. It comes with practice, and also depends on what type of story you're writing. An action-packed adventure will most likely be faster paced overall than a suspenseful mystery, for example.

Be aware of pace, and have a play with it. Ease back on a scene and give your character (and your reader) a chance to breathe, or go at a scene full throttle, if the action demands it.

WHEN THE STORY GETS STUCK

Sometimes, a story runs out of steam. You might have written pages and pages of fabulous story, and then, for some reason, it stops. There are lots of reasons why this might happen, and here are a few common ones.

If you're struggling to concentrate, the first thing to do is probably take a break. We can be thinking so hard about our story that we can't see the woods for the trees, as the saying goes. Go for a walk, read a book, do some sport, bake a cake—just as long as you do something different. Having said that, sometimes doing something different won't be enough. I know that occasionally I have had to set the story to one side until I feel able to concentrate again—and that's perfectly OK. Remember, don't be too hard on yourself. I'm hoping that you're writing for fun, and if it stops being fun, stop doing it for a bit.

You haven't got the brain-space to concentrate

The story feels boring or you're not enjoying writing this particular bit

If you're not enjoying writing a section, or it feels boring, leave that bit! When I'm struggling, I write something really simple like 'Aaaargh!' or 'She gets dressed' there and move on to the next bit that I *do* want to write or can picture more clearly in my head. I have to go back to the stuck bit at *some* point, but by then I might feel better about it, or have thought of a way to make it more exciting. Sometimes, bits I feel are boring end up being taken out of the story altogether, because in the end *they're not important*.

For example, we don't necessarily need to know that Millicent ate cereal, toast with raspberry jam, two boiled eggs, and three sausages for breakfast; just telling the reader she ate breakfast might be enough.

If you've run out of ideas or can't see what happens next, kickstart your brain by asking questions. What would happen if ... ? Or make your character do something unexpected. Let something unexpected happen *to* them. Even better, you could ask your character what happens next. Now that last one sounds a bit barmy, I admit, but I've written conversations with my characters before now, and they've ended up telling me what should be happening—it's a kind of subconscious way of allowing your writer's head to bring out into the open the things that are bubbling under the surface.

You've run out of ideas and can't see what comes next

If something's not working out in the plot, the approach is similar to having run out of ideas. Except this time, you're asking yourself (and maybe the characters) questions not to find something new to include, but to work out how to make things right. Imagine a whodunnit for example—you might realise that your thief couldn't possibly have been waiting at home for the police to arrive, ten miles away from the scene of the crime, because they didn't have any transport and the police would have reached the thief's home first. Will you change where the thief went? Give them a car to get home quicker? Maybe the police will have to visit the next day? Play around with some ideas, until you find one that works. Then check it doesn't affect anything else in the story, because if you give the thief a car to drive, are they—for example—even old enough to drive ... ?

Something's not working out in the plot

If you start to think that what you are writing is rubbish—and I've had moments like this—it may well be that it's not the best writing you've ever done. But when you look closely at that

You tell yourself it's rubbish

writing, you will find bits that are better than you thought they were. Remember that whenever you start to write a story, it *will* be rough round the edges to begin with. *No one* writes a perfect first draft.

More often than not, it's the Doubt Demon who puts the idea you're rubbish into your head.

Lots of writers have this little demon, who criticises them and tells them they're no good—even bestselling authors! Tell that little demon to get lost, and keep on writing. Given time, your writing ability *and* your confidence will grow and you won't feel like this as often, but before then you have to remind yourself that you *can* write and that you're allowed not to write perfectly or well, especially when you're still working things out.

BREAKING IT UP—
CHAPTERS

Usually, a short story doesn't need chapters, but it may use an extra line break or an asterisk to indicate a shift of scene or character's point of view.

Some longer stories don't have chapters, either. Remember I mentioned Terry Pratchett? He rarely used chapters in his novels; he tended to stick to line breaks. But each line break warned the reader that a change was coming . . .

Longer stories usually benefit from breaking the story into chapters, though. When I'm working out a novel's story, I tend to mark in where I think chapter breaks will be, but never fix them until the story is completely finished.

Chapters tend to be used to indicate a major change of location, a change in point of view where there are multiple narrators (more on these later), a passage of time, or to deliberately leave the reader on a cliffhanger.

Chapters can be different lengths. There *are* some writers who aim to make their chapters all a certain number of pages long, or have so many words in them, but I tend to work more on gut feeling. Where does it feel there is a natural break in the story? This means that my chapter lengths are quite varied—some are as short as a single page! Others are much longer as I write my characters through certain scenes.

A chapter break is a good way of cutting out lots of unnecessary detail sometimes. Instead of, for example, writing about the three weeks it took your characters to get from A to B, you could finish one chapter with them setting off, and begin the next with them arriving at their destination. Something like this . . .

"Are we ready?" Harold glanced around at his friends. "Then let's go."

CHAPTER 7

It had been a long, hard three weeks. Three weeks of walking in all weathers while their feet blistered and hardened. Three weeks of rationing their food and going to bed hungry. Three weeks of sleeping under the stars, wondering how much longer it would be before they saw the spires of Jerunt's famous cathedral and knew they had arrived.

"There they are!"

Harold's shout made everyone look up.

Or what about a chapter break where one chapter finishes on a cliffhanger, and the next begins with a change of character?

As the dragon's claws tore through the roof, Tara threw her arms over her head and screamed.

CHAPTER 4

"Tara! Tara, where are you?" Frank scrambled over the debris that had once been his home, dragging at the broken branches that used to be a roof.

Don't leave the reader on a cliffhanger too often though, or it begins to lose its impact. And make sure it really *is* a cliffhanger moment, not a place where you've artificially stopped in the middle of the action and the chapter should really carry on . . .

Play with chapters if you feel you need them, and see whether you can detect where that natural break needs to happen. With experience, you'll recognise these places more easily. Sometimes, it'll still be a bit of a struggle. You may find that what you've written at the start of chapter is unnecessary, because the action starts later in. Or that you've added something at the end of one chapter that might actually be better placed at the start of the next.

Chapter breaks always depend on your story . . . and how you have chosen to structure it.

Chapter 5

Creating the Cast—Characters

Have you ever read a story that didn't have any characters in it? I haven't. I mean, the characters weren't always *people*—they might have been animals, or aliens, or werewolves, even a house on one occasion—but they were always characters.

Coming up with a character

Characters are essential, and writing them is one of the things I love most about starting a new story. I'm going to suggest some ways to help you create a character from scratch. I've used all of them either on their own or in combination, but I get on better with some more than others. Like a lot of things in writing, try a few and see which work best for you; I've given you the ideas in an order which will help you to develop your character, but if you prefer to think of a name first and work from there, go for it!

Hopefully, by the time you get to the end of this section, you'll have at least one new character to drop into a story.

FIND A PICTURE

When I first started writing seriously and needed a character, I'd have an idea about who I wanted in my story: a boy with red hair, for example. But I couldn't always 'see' what this person looked like in my head. So, I'd look in magazines or on the internet until I found a picture of a boy with red hair who looked like someone I'd like to write about. Often, I'd be working on gut feeling, because there'd be something about the person in the picture that drew me to them. Once I'd printed or cut the picture out, I had a reference to work from.

Try it yourself. Flick through a magazine or search the internet for a picture of someone you'd quite like to write about. It could be a photograph or a drawing. If you want to be more specific, choose from a more limited range of options like teacher, wizard, peasant, queen, police, or alien, for example. Or select an age or physical characteristic, and search for something like 'old woman', or 'man with braided hair'.

Remember to print the picture or cut it out of the magazine so you have it to refer to as you're writing about them.

GET PHYSICAL

Is your character tall or short? Are they young or old? What gender are they? What are they wearing? What colour are their eyes? Do they have a scar or a wooden leg? Do they have one head—or two?

You get the idea.

So now, write a list of physical characteristics for a character, using either your imagination or the picture you've found. Bear in mind that if you are using a picture and it only shows part of the person, you'll have to use your imagination to flesh out the bits you can't see. Of course if you are using only your imagination, you'll have to think of *everything*.

Be as specific and detailed as you like, but don't worry about writing a full description unless you want to. A list of characteristics will do the job just as well. Either way, once you've done it, you'll know an awful lot about what your character looks like.

BEHAVIOUR

Having a description of what they look like is great, but it doesn't give you an idea of what the character is actually *like*. Do they prefer cats to dogs? Are they happy? Mean? Generous? Scared of spiders?

You could ask questions like these and build up a deeper picture of your character and of how they might behave in a given situation. Your character's favourite colour is pink? How would they behave in a room where everything in it is pink? What if they hate pink? How would they behave in the same situation?

What are their favourite foods? Who are their friends? Their enemies? What do they want most in life? What do they fear?

Sometimes, how the character is going to behave is vital to the plot—if they are scared of spiders and will have to battle the Giant Eight-legged Beast of Birmingham in your story, then that's going to be important to know from the start!

But sometimes you *don't* know how a character is going to behave. You have to write about them and get to know them better, before they start to show the things they are scared of or want most or prefer. When they do, that's when the character really starts to come alive within the story world you've created, and you can work with them to build your story.

GOOD or BAD?

Lots of characters tend to be good or bad. When we begin to write, good characters are often very good, and bad ones very bad, but in real life, no-one is entirely good or entirely bad.

Imagine a perfect person—they do everything right, all the time. They never get angry or upset, because life is wonderful. Now imagine the opposite—someone who is *so* bad, they really ought to be locked away so they can't hurt or upset anyone—ever!

Problem is, if all the baddies were locked away, and all the goodies live good lives, we've got nothing to write about!

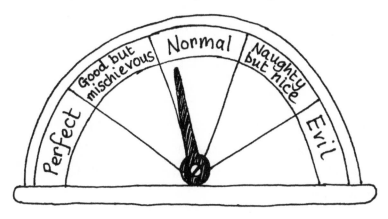

That's because some of the most memorable characters are those which are a mixture of good *and* bad. And honestly, that's what most people are in real life—I think very few people deliberately set out to be bad, but the circumstances they find themselves in might make them do things that we'd consider not to be good. Good people sometimes tell lies. Good people still get angry at times and throw things. As for baddies . . . well, even a villain must have a soft spot somewhere. They might well want to rule the country and throw everyone who disagrees with them into jail—but their pet cat, Fluffy, sleeps on a bed of feathers and eats salmon every day for dinner.

Can you see how that instantly makes both the good and bad characters more like us? I bet we've all done things we wish we hadn't, or wished we'd been better than we were. There might even have been times when we wished we could do something *really* naughty . . . We are human—and human characteristics like jealousy, anger, fear, love, hope, selfishness, greed, or helpfulness will help a reader to connect to the character you've created. Even if they are an alien or a talking animal . . .

NAMES

Names can be powerful. They can create a picture in a reader's head even before you show them what the character looks like! Here are a few names—what kind of person do *you* think they are?

Jim Smith

Lady Ponsonby-Smythe

Henry Humdinger

Margoletta Mystanton

Arto Krunkle

Kylie-Louise Broaden

Here's what I think:

Lady Ponsonby-Smythe is posh. She lives with her poodle, Mimi, in a grand mansion with pink marble floors and likes to call everyone 'Dah-link'!

Jim Smith is quite ordinary, the kind of person who lives quietly, goes shopping every Thursday, does the suduko puzzle in the paper, and grows beans in his back garden.

Henry Humdinger . . . hmm . . . he's something exciting like an inventor. 'Henry Humdinger's Marvellous Jam-making Machine'!

Margoletta Mystanton–goodness! She's an enchantress, with long black hair and grey eyes, who always wears sequinned robes when she casts her spells.

Arto Krunkle is from Zabalda, and he's a thief, wanted for stealing the Ring of Alabam from the Castle of Tears.

Kylie-Louise Broaden is a schoolgirl who is mad about the boyband BettaBoyz, and she's doing odd jobs to earn enough money to buy a ticket to their next concert.

Of course, names can also be used to surprise the reader. Lord Tattle could actually be the leader of a gang of thieves. And Richard Jones might sound ordinary, but actually, he's a super-spy.

If you're ever stuck for a name, try out a name finder. They have hundreds of names in all sorts of languages, will tell you whether they are suitable for boys or girls or both, and sometimes even what the names mean. I play with these a lot! If you find a name you like, try it out on your character—but don't worry if it doesn't seem to suit them. My characters sometimes try on two or three names until one clicks and I know who I'm writing about. And some names *definitely* sound better on a baddie than a goodie . . .

Have fun with them!

USING REAL PEOPLE

Some stories include real people, either living or dead. Let's deal with the dead ones first.

If you wanted to write a time-travelling story, and went back in time to meet Einstein, then there are certain things that the reader will expect of Einstein in the story because he is such a well-known historical figure. If you choose to make your story realistic and have him devise the Theory of Relativity over the course of the story, you'll need to get at least some of the facts right. But if, for example, you want to imagine Einstein on a spaceship, you've got a bit more freedom to be inventive!

Using real people who are still alive is more of a problem. If you write the story in such a way that your Great-Auntie Mavis recognises the horrible tea pot collection in your story as hers, she might not be too happy. In the same way, if you wrote about the behaviour of a friend in such detail that they—and others—would recognise themself, they would likely be very upset.

If you speak badly of anyone—living or dead—there is a risk that you could get into serious trouble. It's probably wiser and safer to stick to using them as inspiration for characters rather than having them appear in your story as their real selves. It sounds really sneaky, but as a writer you learn to hide this kind of real-people-inspiration in plain sight, especially if it is something that is not very complimentary to the person.

Instead of giving your character a collection of teapots like Great-Auntie Mavis's, you make it one of Toby jugs, which are actually funny pottery jugs with ugly faces on them!

Instead of writing about the time your friend accidentally knocked your birthday cake off the table, you make a character deliberately knock a wedding cake over. If you're being bullied and you want the bully in your story to get their comeuppance, don't write that they are tall with blonde hair if they are—make them short and dark.

Even when you aren't using real people, there is a slim chance that someone you know will still think you've written about them; there is more than one bully in the world. There are lots of people who collect weird things. And I'm sure more than one celebration cake has been knocked over.

Just think very, very carefully before you use real people in your story . . .

CHARACTER
QUESTIONNAIRE

One way to keep track of your character's characteristics is to fill in a Character Questionnaire, because if you have difficulties remembering, you might forget that a character's eyes are supposed to be blue, not brown. Or that they hate ice cream, so they shouldn't be eating it halfway through the story.

Coming up at the end of this section is an example of a character questionnaire with some of the characteristics you might want to record. Of course you can tailor the questions to suit your story, because it may not be necessary to know what their favourite colour or favourite meal is.

Although, if Gertie hates the colour orange and loves purple, and yet she's always dressed in orange and her twin sister in purple, you might want to make a note of that for when they go shopping together.

And if your story is about Lord Artelly-Port's adventure to find the last tin of baked beans in existence, you may want to record that he can't imagine living without beans on toast . . .

If you have a large cast of characters in your story, you could complete a questionnaire for each of them, and store them in character files.

Name: EXAMPLE

Age: CHARACTER

Gender/Species: QUESTIONNAIRE

What colour eyes/hair?

What's distinctive about them? (Scars, special
powers, etc)

Where do they live?

What do they do if they have a job?

What do they enjoy most in all the world?

Who are their friends?

Who are their enemies?

What are they most scared of?

What do they want more than anything?

What is their most prized possession?

What do they always have in their pocket?

DEVELOPING A CHARACTER

In real life, people are changed by what happens to them,
what they experience. In the same way, over the course of
a story, characters change because they are experiencing
events in the story that will leave a lasting impression on
them. This will be especially true of your main character(s).

They may end up physically altered thanks to what they've
experienced, and now possess an interesting scar after the
fiercest of battles. Perhaps the magic spell backfired and
they've now got permanently blue hair.

They will most certainly have grown as a person. They've found out more about the world and their place in it. Perhaps they've discovered they aren't as afraid of the dark as they believed they were, or that they do have what it takes to become chief of the tribe.

Let's face it, if everything they've gone through in the story hasn't made any difference to them, then the story probably won't have made a difference to the reader, either. The reader has invested in the adventures of the character and wants to see them succeed or get their come-uppance—don't disappoint.

TAKE AWAY WHAT THEY WANT, AND GIVE THEM WHAT THEY FEAR

If we were talking about real people, you would probably feel terrible if I told you to be deliberately horrible to them. It's natural not to want to take something precious away from someone, or put them into a situation where they are going to be frightened or that they may want to avoid. But if you can bear to do it to the characters in your story, it can make things really interesting. For example:

If your character really, really wants to be rich, and they lose all their money . . . what will they do?

If David is afraid of the dark, but the only way to rescue the lost dog is to go into the tunnel where the barking's coming from . . . what will he do?

If Elyza is a witch who wants to heal people, but magic is forbidden in her land . . . what will she do?

It can feel odd to treat characters this way, but it's something you need to get used to. Think of the expression 'It's character building.' It means people sometimes come out of a bad situation stronger, more confident, and possibly with new skills . . . The same is true when your characters face a situation that is hard or difficult for them.

The way we do this in our stories is to create conflict.

Conflict doesn't just mean war and fighting. It could be any situation where characters want opposing things, have difficult decisions to make or problems to solve, and it's how our characters react to these things that will help to shape the story we're building.

Conflict in this sense might make characters argue over the best route to take to the train station. It might give them a situation where they have to discover if they have the strength to overcome their fear of the dark, or do the right thing even if it means risking punishment. It could even be the tug of conscience when lying to a friend.

Remember that you might be writing your characters into these situations—but you can also write your characters out of them, too. What's important is thinking about how going through that particular form of conflict will affect your character and remember to show your reader how they change as a result.

Chapter 6
Whose story is it?
Points of View

When you write a story, *you* tell it, right?

Not really.

What actually happens is that you—as the author and creator of the story—get to choose who tells it. You are the *author*, but not necessarily the *narrator*.

Imagine for a moment, the following scene. A dragon is sitting on a huge pile of treasure in its den. A sword-wielding dragonslayer has just arrived to kill the dragon, but unbeknown to both of them, a young thief has joined them from the entrance to a secret passage.

Now, we have three characters who could tell the reader what happens in this scene. One of them will become our narrator, our storyteller. It will be their point of view (POV) we see the scene from—dragon's, dragonslayer's, or thief's. Not only that, but we can also choose to write from a first, second, or third person perspective for any of these characters.

Let me try and explain.

First person is written with words like I, me, myself. It puts the reader firmly into the head of a character and sees the world through their eyes.

So to continue with our dragon's den example:

The cave entrance was scorched, with deep gouges visible in the rock. I pulled Scalecutter slowly from its scabbard, the metal glinting red in the light of the sunset. Gripping the hilt tightly in both hands, I took a deep breath. Then I took my first step towards my destiny.

The reader is entering the cave with the dragonslayer, feeling their feelings, seeing what they are seeing.

Third person is written with words like they, he, she, it. It can be written from a limited or omniscient–see-all–view.

Limited (which I tend to write in most frequently) would sound something like . . .

Eralta stared in disbelief at the tiny figure that had dared to enter her domain. At least this one hadn't bothered with the hard shiny coverings that usually got stuck in her teeth when she ate intruders that failed to kill her. She reared up, opened her mouth, and shot a burst of flame towards the ceiling.

You're imagining yourself as the dragon, but perhaps watching the scene a little more than being immersed in it.

Omniscient, or see-all, would allow us to view all the characters' thoughts or feelings in a moment. So, we might write . . .

Eralta reared up, angry at the intrusion, her scaly belly studded with golden coins and jewels. The slayer froze at the sight, torn between admiration for such a glorious beast, and terror of the same. Unnoticed, the thief crept closer to the edge of the treasure pile, thanking her lucky stars for the unexpected distraction.

If the story had been told with, say, different characters telling different parts, and this is the point where their different stories all come together in one place, the reader is caught up almost as a god, watching what happens next.

Second person is generally not used for stories, but it uses words like you and yours, and addresses the reader directly. You're not just experiencing what the character experiences—you *are* the character. Which might mean writing . . .

You blow out your lantern and creep along the last bit of the tunnel, using only the reflected golden light to guide you. When you see the dragon rear up, you cringe, expecting its fiery breath to be the last thing you'll ever feel. But then you spot the other intruder—the slayer—standing at the entrance to the den.

This is a point of view more often used for instructions, although books where readers choose what happens next in the story tend to use it a lot!

When writing stories, you tend to pick one POV and stick to it, although in longer stories you might find that an author switches between different characters' POVs for longer sections or different chapters. It depends entirely on the plot.

Problems with **POV**

Most writers use a first or third person limited viewpoint for their narrator, and there are some issues to look out for. Both of these POVs draw your reader much closer to the character who is telling the story, but that also means that the reader can't know anything that the character doesn't know, feel anything other than what they feel, or see what they can't see. And they can't know what other characters are thinking, either. Read this little section, written from Eralta's POV:

Eralta narrowed her eyes to slits as the unnoticed thief continued to creep behind her back. The dragonslayer was scared almost witless, wondering whether his sword was going to be enough for the job in front of him. She breathed a thick plume of steam in his direction.

Now, there's actually no way our dragon, Eralta, could know that the thief was still creeping, because the author has told the reader that they were unnoticed, and more importantly, Eralta *can't actually see her*! Not unless she's got eyes in the back of her head, anyway. And Eralta can't know what the slayer's thinking either, unless you (as the writer) decided from the start that she's a mind-reading dragon. We jumped into the slayer's head—only for a moment—but it was enough. The author can make Eralta guess that the slayer is scared and wondering about his sword, but can't make her know for sure. Writers call this head-hopping.

These head-hops and impossible-to-see/know situations tend to pull the reader out of your story if they are imagining themselves to be Eralta the dragon. And that doesn't make for a story that flows well.

Chapter 7

Punctuation, tense, and grammar

As I said before, I am not a teacher. Whole books have been written by other people about punctuation and grammar and the like, so I'm not going to cover it in this book. And you might actually know more about the theory than I do!

But I will remind you here to do your best to . . .

Make sure you know which tense you are writing in, and make sure you stick to it!

Use punctuation correctly.

Obey the grammar rules. (Unless you're writing dialogue—what's spoken is not usually grammatically correct!)

Get help on this if you need it.

Chapter 8

He said, she said— Dialogue

I don't think I've ever read a story that didn't have any talking at all in it. Think about how much we talk to each other in real life! Speech in stories has an important function, because it's not just chatting between characters, it's there to help move the story forward by what it tells the reader.

(Remember that communication is not restricted to speech. Consider sign language, or how a dog barks or growls, or morse code, for example.)

In this section, I'm going to deal only with how characters speak to each other.

HOW TO WRITE SPEECH

Speech is *always* written inside speech marks. (There are some books that break this rule, but they are few and far between and honestly, quite difficult to read in my experience).

Now, I refer to them as speech marks because that's how most people in the UK refer to them. In the US they're called quotation marks and you may also see them referred to as inverted commas. What's important is that it's the thing in written dialogue that indicates these words are being spoken by a character.

In school, I was taught to use "double" speech marks, or 66 at the start and 99 at the finish of the speech:

"Hello!"

Can you see what I mean about the numbers? Some books use 'single' speech marks, which only gives us a 6 and a 9.

'Hello!'

When you write dialogue it doesn't really matter whether you use single or double speech marks, as long as they are there, you use the same kind all through one story, and they're the right way round when you do. When you write dialogue, it's important to know what the accepted norm is for speech marks. For example, in the UK, people will use double *or* single speech marks, making sure they use just one kind consistently throughout the story. In the US, double marks are always used. (Certain fonts on the computer don't show the way round quite so clearly, so be careful if you are using an unusual font. And if you are writing by hand, you don't have to use 6s and 9s—angled straight lines will do.)

All punctuation goes *inside* the speech marks, which means a simple conversation between two people would be written:

"Hello."
"How are you?"
"Don't touch that!"
"I wasn't going to, honest."

Each new line indicates a different person speaking, but at the moment, we don't know who's saying what.

DIALOGUE TAGS

To identify the speakers, we add what writers call dialogue tags. At their simplest, these are written *Name said*, or *said Name*:

"Hello," Kim said.
"How are you?" said John.

'Said' is the best way of identifying or tagging the person who's speaking as it's transparent to the reader–they don't tend to notice it. It's also the simplest verb you can use to make that identification obvious.

PING PONG DIALOGUE

Sometimes, a conversation is longer and moves back and forth between two, three, or maybe even more characters. Both of the following examples are ping-pong dialogue–it goes back and forth between two people like a game of table tennis.

"Hello," said Kim.
"How are you," said John.
"Don't touch that," Kim said.
"I wasn't going to," John said.
"Yes, you were," Kim said.
"Well, I wanted to see if it was real," John said.

Said isn't exactly invisible here, is it? Repeated so many times, it gets a bit distracting. Imagine what it would be like if Kim and John talked for longer and we had to keep writing 'said'. So let's try taking away some and see if it makes it less distracting.

"Hello," Kim said.
"How are you?" John said.
"Don't touch that!"
"I wasn't going to."
"Yes, you were."
"Well, I wanted to see if it was real."
"It is."
"How can you be sure? It's huge."
"It's been tested. It's definitely real."
"How much is it worth?"
"Ooh, millions I should think."

Now, without going back to the start of the conversation to check, who said "Ooh, millions I should think?"

It's easy to forget who's speaking in a conversation this long with no dialogue tags, isn't it? If the dialogue wasn't as long, we might have gotten away with it, but as it stands—or even longer—without reminding the reader who's saying what, things can get very confusing.

So, what can we do as authors to avoid slipping into ping pong dialogue with too many 'saids' or none at all? We *could* help the reader by making things more interesting, and change the dialogue tag from 'said' to something else while still using the character's names. However, it is better to use the simplest verb possible to get the meaning across to the reader.

For example:

"I wasn't going to touch it, honest," John whispered.

Try and steer clear of using fancy alternatives to 'said'. My thesaurus has two pages filled with a list containing thirty-four alternatives to 'said', but I certainly wouldn't try and use all of them! If I did, I'd certainly be avoiding the use of 'said', but it's very easy to go over the top and I wouldn't necessarily be using the most appropriate verb. (Opined? Expostulated? No, I'm not sure what they mean, either!) It's considered to be an obvious sign of an inexperienced author if they frequently use anything other than the simplest said-related verbs as dialogue tags. There *are* times when you might need something more extravagant, but if so, use it only when *absolutely* necessary. Not every dialogue tag has to be different.

It is far better to make it obvious *how* the words are spoken by the choice of words and how they are used by the speaker. If you as the author have to *tell* the reader how something is being said, then the words you have made your character speak probably haven't expressed fully what you wanted to get across.

"Don't touch that!" Kim yelled loudly.
"I wasn't going to," John whispered quietly.

We know that yelling is usually loud, and whispering is usually quiet—there is no need to add this information because the choice of yelled and whispered implies those things.

In the same way, be careful about using dialogue tags where the verb cannot possibly be applied to speech. You cannot, for example, sneer or laugh words:

"You are nothing more than a worm," Larry sneered.
"What on earth are you wearing?" Sheila laughed.

We can still use those verbs, but we have to use them differently, which moves us nicely onto . . .

ACTION TAGS

Another very clever way to identify *who* is speaking is to use an action tag. So, if we rewrote Larry and Sheila's dialogue . . .

Larry sneered. "You are nothing more than a worm."
Sheila laughed. "What on earth are you wearing?"

Let's go back to a little bit of Kim and John's conversation . . .

Kim wagged a finger at him. "Yes, you were."
"Well, I wanted to see if it was real." John stepped away from the giant jewel.

See how describing an action links the speech to the character? We now know who's speaking *and* we know something of what they're doing at the same time. Like a two-for-the-price-of-one deal!

By using a combination of dialogue and action tags, with sometimes no tags at all, the dialogue starts to come alive. It's more than people speaking to each other. It's got action and purpose, and drives the scene or story on. Read the whole conversation again . . .

"Hello," Kim called, hanging up on her coat.
"How are you?"

Kim would have answered, but what she saw when she turned round made her shout a warning. "Don't touch that!"

John snatched his hand away. "I wasn't going to."

Kim wagged a finger at him. "Yes, you were."

"Well, I wanted to see if it was real." John stepped away from the giant jewel.

"It is."

"How can you be sure? It's huge."

"It's been tested," Kim said. "It's definitely real."

"How much is it worth?"

She shrugged. "Ooh, millions I should think."

Having read that, find a story you've enjoyed and turn to a page where there is a fair amount of dialogue. Read it through, paying attention to how the author uses speech and action tags.

Now have a go for yourself. Pick one of the following situations and write a short conversation for the people involved in it. Don't have too many people—two or three only.

A student explaining to their teacher why their homework hasn't been done.

An argument over who ate the last chocolate biscuit.

Trying to encourage someone to do something they don't want to do.

A visitor to town, asking for directions.

A customer complaining about their meal in a restaurant.

UM . . . ERR . . .

If you sit and listen to people talking, you'll soon discover that real speech has lots of 'um' and 'err' moments in it. If we wrote dialogue in stories how we speak in life, then most books would be a lot, *lot* longer than they are, because pages would be taken up with umms and ahhs and all sort of other noises we make without realising.

You may well find an umm or err moment in dialogue in a story, but usually that's because the author is using it deliberately, most often to make the character hesitate. It's there for a reason.

Written dialogue is written for effect—it adds something to the story—and should be realistic, but with all the hesitation and strange noises removed. Remember; dialogue should exist to move the story on.

EEEE BY GUM!

Depending on where you're from, you might have an accent when you talk.

You might be from Yorkshire . . . 'By 'eck, does tha know abowt t'shop closin' early?'

Or Scotland . . . 'Och aye the noo! There's juice loose aboot this hoose!'

Or you might be Australian . . . 'G'day mate! How's about a barbie on the beach?'

(With apologies to people who live in Yorkshire, Scotland, or Australia!)

If it's done well, you can hear the accent when reading in your head, or you can sound like someone else entirely when you read the words aloud. The best author I've discovered so far for accents is called Brian Jacques, who wrote the Redwall series of books. His first stories were written when he was a milkman and made friends with children who went to a school for the blind which he delivered milk to. They must have loved to hear about his talking animals, because he gave them all accents and distinct ways of speaking when he read the books to them. The hares were soldiers, and spoke very 'Tally ho! Right you are, old chap! No carrots, what?' for example. Other animals talked with a soft country accent, 'That be clearer'n broit summer morn, thankee, zurr.' It's very clever and sounds wonderful read aloud if you say what you see!

Although hard to do well, with a bit of practise you can sprinkle little bits of accent through your dialogue. Do be careful though—writing in an accent for everything a character says can make the reader work really hard to understand what's actually being said.

What kind of accents are these?

"'Ow can you let that 'appen?"
"Ze Doctor vill see you soon."
"'Ere, guvnor! Wot you doin'?"
"I've been down the valley, boyo, and it's raining."

(In case you were wondering, they're my attempts at French, German, Cockney, and Welsh! With even more apologies . . .)

Of course, accents don't have to be from just a different country, or even from a region. They could exist between different types or classes of people. Think about how some people speak more formally than others for example.

EXPLAINING

One thing characters don't do in written dialogue is explain things that they would never explain in real life. So, for example, you wouldn't have a conversation that goes like this:

"Of course, I only became your friend at first because you are incredibly rich," Nadia said.

"And you thought that I would pay for everything because I am such a generous person. But it wasn't long before you liked me simply because of my amazing personality, and money didn't come into it any more," Greg replied.

I mean, this might pass if these friends are having a joke, but you wouldn't usually talk to a friend in an everyday conversation like this, would you? You *know* why you're friends—you don't need to *tell* each other why.

If the information contained in the speech is important to the story you're writing, then perhaps you actually need to write the scene where Greg and Nadia meet.

KEEPING IT REAL

When you have characters speak in your story, it needs to sound realistic. We've already touched on that and said we need to miss out the umms and errs, and we need to avoid characters explaining to each other, but there's another way that dialogue can fail to sound realistic.

This happens when the author writes all the characters' dialogue the same way, (as though they are the same person), or uses language inappropriate for the character.

The first makes the conversation sound flat and monotone because everyone in the story speaks the same way. There's no variation in tone or style between characters.

"I'm popping down to the shops," Kate said to her grandpa. "Would you like me to fetch anything?"

"I'd like a bag of smoky bacon crisps and a newspaper, please. I'll pop into the garden while you're gone," Sid replied.

"Alright. I'll see you when I get back."

That conversation is realistic in that we can imagine Kate offering to fetch something as a favour for her Grandpa. But if we assume Kate is a teenager and change how she speaks, see how it alters the feel of the dialogue:

"I'm goin' out," Kate said. "You want anything?"

"I'd like a bag of smoky bacon crisps and a newspaper, please. I'll pop into the garden while you're gone," her Grandpa Sid replied.

"'Kay. See ya later."

What about if the language is inappropriate for a character?

"Release my arm this instant, you rogue," snapped the thief.

"Not until you hand back my purse," Lady Tyler replied.

Now, unless the thief in question is actually someone of a similar social standing to Lady Tyler, I'd be much more likely to believe the conversation if it went something like . . .

"Gerroff!" snapped the thief.

"Not until you hand back my purse," Lady Tyler replied.

Try, as much as you can, to make character's voices distinct, appropriate, and realistic.

Chapter 9
Location, location, location—
Building worlds

A story always takes place *somewhere,* and writing about the place where the story happens can be so important in setting the mood of the story, or to give the characters a world to live in.

Creating this world is called world building, and the aim is to make the reader really believe in the place or places that they read about—even if the only place they do exist is in the author's head!

Real places

I have to say that world building is something I really enjoy. I like my imaginary worlds much more than the real one sometimes, and I can have floating cities or flying cars or three suns if I want them. But worlds and places don't always have to come from your imagination, and some writers find it hard to imagine completely new ones.

It is just as good to use real places, whether for inspiration or because your story is set in say, Covent Garden in London, or the Sahara Desert, or beside Lake Tekapo in New Zealand. (Lake Tekapo is beautiful—the water is bright turquoise!) If you haven't heard of these places, why not do some research and find out about them?

Think of somewhere you know really well—can you see it in your head? It might be a school classroom, a park, your bedroom, a grandparent's house. Imagine yourself in that place now, and write about it.

Did you find it relatively easy to do, because you'd been there and could remember what it was like? Good.

I have strong memories of my Grandma's house:

In Grandma's house there was a small bedroom and a lounge to the front of the house, stairs in the middle, and the kitchen to the back. A corridor led to the back door—off it was the pantry, the coal store, and a toilet. Upstairs were two bedrooms, front and back, and a loft store under the eaves. Grandma had coal fires in the four main rooms. She also had a huge dining table with five legs, a sideboard, and a cabinet with photos of family on top of it.

Now, what I've written isn't a very detailed description, and it sticks to the facts. It probably sounds a bit old fashioned (it was!) but it doesn't really tell you much about how it felt to be in the house, does it?

How does your piece of writing compare? Did you stick to the basic facts, or describe things in more detail?

To build a world that your reader can imagine and believe in, we probably need a little bit more. Let's visit Grandma's house again . . .

In the winter, there'd be a roaring coal fire in the lounge and a smaller one in the kitchen. In the lounge, Grandma's chair was right beside the fire, next to the sideboard which was her pride and joy and had all the best dinner plates inside it. The dining table was huge, heavy, and a dark wood, and we used to play forts underneath it. Grandma cooked on the open fire in the kitchen most days, and only used the oven when family visited. The pantry was filled with jams and cakes she'd made, and the shelves were covered in bits of wrapping paper.

Right, we're getting some more detail in there now. Something of Grandma is beginning to colour the picture as well. If you haven't done it already, look back at what you've written about your place. Can you add this extra level of detail?

Now as you read what I wrote, you might have felt as though you were looking around Grandma's house with me. Sight is just one of our senses, though—we have four more we could use in our stories to make places come alive. What about sound, taste, smell, and touch? By describing a place and using *all* the senses, we can try to put the reader right into the body of the character. Imagine, then, a very much younger Squidge, at Grandma's now . . .

The fire in the lounge would sometimes blaze so fiercely, I could believe I was being cooked. And yet any bit of me facing away from the fire would be cold from the draught pulled by the same flames. The coal would rumble into the grate when it was added, the dust bitter in my nose until the meatiness of Grandma's Sunday Roast wafted in from the kitchen to cover it up. The fire would glow cherry red, gently hissing as recently added damp coal dried out. Sometimes it would spit and crackle and shoot sparks out onto the hearth rug, making Dad jump up and rub at the place where they'd landed with a coin until the carpet wasn't smouldering any more. The sickly sweetness of Bonfire Toffee and the nuttiness of roasted chestnuts always take me back to Grandma's lounge and sitting by her fireplace.

Were you there with me? Could you feel the heat of the fire on your face? Taste the toffee? Hear the fire crackling? Smell the roast beef cooking?

Effective world building brings the reader right into the place … makes it believable and real. Take another look at the place you began writing about. How can you write with your senses to transport us there?

Imaginary places

Lots of stories are set in places that don't actually exist. Like in a school for wizards and witches for example, or on another planet. In a spaceship. Deep among the streets of a floating city. And yet, when we read the stories, we believe that they *do* exist. There's a posh term for this; suspension of disbelief. It basically means that you know it can't possibly be real, but it's been written to seem so real, you *do* believe and enjoy it.

Sometimes, an imaginary place is inspired by a real one. A city built on a series of canals may well be based on Venice. A haunted house may be based on a photograph of a derelict mansion. The desert on an imaginary planet may well be based on a real one on Earth. Sometimes readers need a bit of something familiar that they can relate to, to anchor them in an imaginary place.

Working mostly from your imagination—touches based on real life *are* allowed!—try describing one of the following places. Remember to use your senses to help describe it if you can.

Have fun, and see what you can come up with.

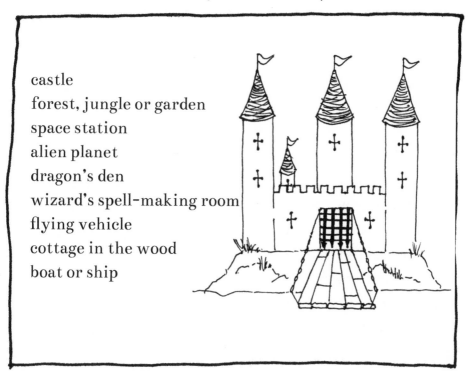

castle
forest, jungle or garden
space station
alien planet
dragon's den
wizard's spell-making room
flying vehicle
cottage in the wood
boat or ship

Filling out a fantasy world

If your story is set in the real world, in modern times, then your reader will probably understand most of what you have presented them with, within the setting of the story. They don't have to work too hard to imagine themselves there.

But in an imaginary world, one that only exists in your author's head, you have to show them more than the strange place(s) where it's set. Remember that phrase—suspension of disbelief? You have to fill out this world to make it completely believable, although how far you go into the detail is up to you and probably affected by the length of your story, too.

Some of the ways you can achieve this filling out is to consider things like:

MONEY How do people in your world pay for things? Do they pay or do they trade—three carrots in exchange for a cabbage, or a day's work for a meal? What's the money like? Is it coins, paper, shells? Do your futuristic characters pay with credit chips?

RELIGION A lot of fantasy stories have a belief system of some kind. One of my books features the Triple Gods of Sun, Moon, and Mountain. Other worlds may worship a sacred tree, or only let red-haired women be priests. If it's important to your story and the world you're creating, then the reader needs to know something about it.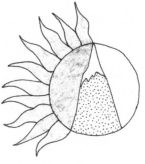

TRANSPORT Is it olde-worlde horse and cart? Spaceships and floating cars? Think about the impact it has on how easy or difficult it is to get around the world you're building.

RULERS AND/OR GOVERNMENT What kind of leaders does your world have? Royalty might rule, or they may be puppets, with the real decision makers hiding in the wings. Or it may be that leaders are made through trials, where only the strongest or cleverest or best at casting spells are allowed to be in charge.

SPECIES AND RACES If you're writing about an alien planet, your characters may be humans who are meeting aliens, or they may well be the aliens themselves. What animals exist in your world? Unicorns? Dragons? Nartalls, a strange beast with three legs and green fur? Talking hedgehogs? You can certainly have fun making these up! If you have different races rather than species, it's pretty much the same approach. Think of a story with people from different lands, and how that might affect their appearance and customs (we're talking worlds within worlds here!).

LANGUAGE I'm not suggesting for one moment that you make up a new language and use it in your story, although some authors have done exactly that. For a start, no reader would be able to understand it unless you also wrote a *How to Speak This Language* book to go with your story. But you *could* add little bits of your made-up language, a bit like we did with accents in dialogue:

"Draxatha," the creature gasped, gesturing at the bottle.

Granta picked it up. "Water? You want water?"

The creature nodded.

Or simply acknowledge that 'Issrayan speech was like music, compared to the harshness of Tradanthan.'

FOOD Is the food recognisable to your reader, even in a made-up world? Are there steaks and roast chicken, toast and jam? Or are there touches of strangeness, with fruit like brisinga berries as well as strawberries and oranges? Or is everything *completely* different, with weird goo or lumps of something hard to which flavour is added? Only you can decide, but remember you have to make it believable for the reader, especially if it's something they have never eaten before or cannot imagine eating. (Poached dragon egg, anyone?)

CLOTHING In most cases, unless everyone in your story is happy being naked, your characters will need something to put on! So is their clothing practical for work or environmental conditions? Is it entirely decorative and a mark of status in society? Is it made of natural materials or space-age fabric?

Beware the info dump

The only problem with all this lovely world building is that, whether it's made up or real, sometimes there's a tendency for authors to explain too much of it to the reader. And when that happens, you're in danger of creating an info dump.

An info dump can be several paragraphs or pages long—worst case, they could even be whole chapters. They occur most often at the start of stories, or when the author is giving the reader lots of information. That's not to say that you can't ever share information; sometimes it's actually essential to explain something of the world that the story is set in, or the technology behind the science, for example.

But the information given should always be secondary to the story: if the story is well told, information can be revealed to the reader through the actions and experiences of the characters, not through a description of the past, for example, or a list of facts.

When an author presents information in the form of an info dump, it usually interrupts the action. Nothing happens. We are pulled out of the story and feel like we're being lectured or told things we don't need to know. It's as though the author is butting in, telling us things we couldn't possibly know from what's currently happening in the story.

Which begs the question, why tell us at all? Here's a short info dump example:

Granta stepped out of the spacetube and stared. The spacetubes had been invented twenty years previously by Dr Teodor Frankin, and were still considered to be the fastest way of getting from Alpha Ten to any of the Class D worlds within five light years of the planet. Travelling by tube was easy. Prior to launch, passengers would book in and be shown to their cryo pods. The necessary monitors would be attached to their bodies and once cryosleep had been initiated, the pods were launched into the tubes. The science behind the tubes was complicated, so most people accepted them without wanting to know how they worked, especially when it meant they could cut journey times by so much. When it was an hour away from its destination, each pod initiated the reanimation sequence, so that on docking, the passengers would be warm, awake, and alert.

All around were the three legged and green furred Nartalls, hurrying about their business. Most of them were carrying envopods on their backs, delivering messages to the poliss as they'd been trained to do.

Did you spot the info dump?

In this example, the detail about space tubes pulled us right out of what was happening to Granta. We don't need that level of detail—and it's probably not important for us to know any of it at this point in the story, either! If it was important, we only really needed to keep what's essential to the scene. Perhaps find a way to show or imply that essential information, and when we do, try to enhance the reader's connection with the character.

So, we might try something like . . .

Granta stepped out of the spacetube and shivered. The pod had warmed him up exactly as it should have done, but after light years of cryosleep he still felt cold somehow whenever he arrived on a Class D world. A Nartall hurried past, the green fur on its back crushed under the bulging envopod it carried. Another message for the poliss, no doubt.

See how that keeps the reader in the moment and the action more? We're given enough information to know that Granta has been asleep and cold for a long time, and he's arrived via spacetube.

If you notice an info dump in your writing, ask yourself:

❶ How much of what you've written is essential for the reader to know right now? If it's not essential, get rid of it—from that place in the story at least.

❷ If the information is essential, how could you rewrite it to show or imply the same thing? Instead of explaining that Tim had overprotective parents, why not show us the argument they had about what time he had to be home by?

❸ How can you use essential information to enhance the emotions of the reader and strengthen their connection to your characters? Maybe don't tell us outright Kara's mum was dead and the circumstances surrounding that time, but let Kara explain for herself; 'I don't know what it feels like. My Mum died when I was seven.'

Remember—make stuff happen! If nothing's happening, you're boring your reader.

Chapter 10

Show and Tell

Sometimes it is enough to tell the reader what happened.

The sun was hot.
Kyle was scared.
It rained all day.

But sometimes we can give our reader a little bit more . . . Let's look at the sun example first.

The sun was hot, and Amy fanned herself while she waited for the prince to arrive.

The fact that the sun is hot is probably not very important here, because your reader might be more interested to know what's going to happen when the prince arrives! Telling the reader that the sun is hot is perhaps enough, in this case.

But what if the fact that it's hot is much more important to a scene?

The sun was hot and there was no water for Amy to drink.

This provides two facts—it's hot, and there's no water. We can imagine that Amy is thirsty, but it feels a little flat to state the information in this way.

But if I'd written it like this . . .

The sun beat down on Amy's head and she prayed for water.

. . . the reader still knows that it's hot, and that Amy is thirsty, but the language used implies that the sun is *really* hot, and Amy's desperation for a drink adds to the picture we're drawing for the reader. We've been shown more than the bare facts, which makes for more interesting reading.

Before we take a look at the second example—Kyle was scared—think about a time when *you* were scared. What did it feel like? What did you do? Or say? When I was scared, I got very shaky, felt sick, and I could feel my heart beating so hard . . .

It might have been a different experience for you. You might have got butterflies in your tummy. You might have wanted to run away. You might have been frozen to the spot, got shivers down your spine, or broken out in a cold sweat . . .

You can use your own experience of being scared to show the reader Kyle's fear without simply telling them he was scared. So instead of writing 'Kyle was scared' we might find that:

Kyle's stomach turned a somersault, then an icy cold shiver ran down his spine.

Kyle's chest tightened and he couldn't breathe.

Kyle tried hard to stop his knees from trembling.

See the difference it makes?

If you feel like it, have a go at 'it rained all day'. Try to *show* the reader the rain, rather than tell them it was raining.

Remember, 'telling' is fine and necessary sometimes. It's not a *bad* thing. But there are times in a story when you can give the reader a better experience and immerse them in the story if you can find a way of sharing the facts by showing them instead. As I'm told sometimes by my editor—'showing and telling depends on context.'

Can you change what you've written to describe the actual feeling, like I've done for Karl? Can you describe what is being heard or seen? Write the question or the thought directly? Here are a few examples:

She felt angry.

This is a perfect example of telling the reader what the character feels. To show that the character is angry, and draw the reader into the moment more, we change it to read something like:

She thumped her fist on the table.

People don't usually act in this way unless they are pretty cross or emphasising a point.

Sometimes, though, 'felt' can show rather than tell:

She felt the heat rise in her cheeks as she clenched her fist.

Only you can decide when to use show or tell. It depends on context—and it's your story, after all.

Chapter 11

Finishing things off —
Editing

Hopefully, if you've stuck with me this far, you'll be well on your way to writing great stories.

You've thought about how to help yourself become a better writer; looked at what kinds of stories you could write; how to plot; how to create characters and write their conversations realistically. You've built a believable world for them to live in—even if it's an imaginary one—and you've given them a problem (or two) to overcome before they get to the end of the story.

You may even have written one or more stories as a result. Hooray! Very well done.

Now you can sit back and relax, right?

Sorry to disappoint, but now is when the hard work *really* begins, because writing a story actually involves a lot of re-writing.

POLISHING

What you've produced to this point is a first draft— you've pieced all your ideas together, and you have a story, but it's likely to be a little rough around the edges. This is the time to read it through again and pick up all the mistakes you've made.

This is a process officially called editing, but you can think of it as polishing if you prefer.

It's probably a stage best approached after you've set your story aside for a few days or weeks so that you can come back to it with fresh eyes.

> Do you know the saying 'Can't see the woods for the trees'? It's true of our stories too—we can get so familiar with what we've written, we can't see the faults in it.

The most obvious things to look for are spelling mistakes, issues with punctuation, and checking for consistency (that your character doesn't have a name change halfway through, for example). Spellings and punctuation have rules, and these need to be obeyed. Suffice to say, this is something you *need* to do.

> As I mentioned earlier, there *are* books that have broken rules in the past, but you have to know the rules before you can break them. If you're starting out, make sure your stories are as good as they can be, especially if you want them to get good marks or you'd like to get them published.

Checking for consistency is also necessary, but there are no rules here as such, because every story is unique. Just make sure that you've stuck to the same place/chosen spelling of a name/hair colour throughout. Otherwise Katherine might become Catherine, Katharine, or even Kathryn, with black/brown/blonde/red hair as the story progresses!

Look out for repeated words, close together in a sentence or paragraph, that weaken the impact of the writing. You'd be amazed how often it happens.

She held up the lamp and its light fell on a dirty boy, crouching in the corner. The boy held up his hands to shield his eyes from the light.

We can polish this little piece and tighten the writing by altering it to:

She held up the lamp and its light fell on a dirty boy, crouching in the corner. The boy raised his hands to shield his eyes.

Discover what your tics are. Tics usually refer to something we do repeatedly—I can't help clicking a pen for example. Tics in writing are the words or phrases you use a lot, sometimes too much. I have a tendency to use 'just' a lot, and have to go back and strike it out, but you might find you write something else.

How about your sentences? Are they all very short and clipped?

He did this. She did that. Then they went somewhere. They got a . . .

Try joining some of them together. But don't join too many. If sentences get too long, consider breaking them up a bit. Most stories don't work very well if they read:

Then he did this and she did that, and then they went somewhere and got this, and then . . .

Look at some of the words you've chosen to use. If you've written 'she ran quickly', would 'she sprinted' be more appropriate? Or 'she dashed'? If your character has a sword, can you be specific? Is it a two-handed broadsword, or a thin fencing blade?

Have your characters become time-travellers, with their actions suddenly changing from past tense to present? 'Timmy turned away and sings the chorus quietly' needs to become either 'Timmy turned away and sang' or 'Timmy turns away and sings' . . .

How's your formatting? I have to admit that when I am working on a first type-up of a story, I don't format it very well at all. So I always have to keep an eye out for paragraph breaks and quotation marks that I've missed. (I also write in my notebooks using abbreviations, so I have to remember to write the full word.)

Look over your dialogue. Does it sound realistic? Have you got speech marks, and are they the right way round?

Have you done any head-hopping between characters—and if so, did you mean to? If you didn't mean to, stop and view the scene through your narrator's eyes. What can they see or guess at? What have you written that they can't possibly know or see?

HAVING A GO . . .

What follows is a genuine story, sent to me after a school visit from someone who was ten years old at the time of writing it. It's reproduced here—unaltered—with their permission. Have a read through it, and feel free to mark the pages with a pencil when you spot anything you think needs a bit of polish . . .

Granny Rainbow's Holiday

It all started with a holiday. Granny Rainbow's holiday to be precise. She was going away to the seaside for a week and Marmaduke was going to stay with old Tom. Marmaduke wanted to go with Granny but the thought of staying with tom and Mrs Fluffy was super-duper exiting.

So off Granny Rainbow went to the seaside; she was looking forwards to meeting up with Grandma Sunshine and Nanny Snow.

At the seaside it was warm and sunny. Maybe because of the wonderful weather, maybe because it was summer, or maybe it was because of Grandma Sunshine's special power; the ability to make the sun come out and to make somewhere pleasantly warm. The only downfall with this was the happier she got the warmer everywhere else got. That's why she stuck with Nanny Snow, who could cool her down, well she was incharge of ice and snow! Well, what about Granny Rainbow? She controls colours of course!

Meanwhile, back at the ranch (meaning back at old Tom's house) a new guy was moving in next door. He was suspicious. His hair was coal and his teeth as yellow as gold. He wore greys, blacks, and dirty blues with a horrible brown and pink golf cap. He wore it backwards. All the animals could sense his evil aura and the way he moved siliently without a sound creeped Tom out. His name? Grampa Raincloud. Granny Rainbow, Grandma Sunshine, and Nanny

Snow's Evil older brother. They were triplets you see,
Granny, Grandma and Nanny, born with colourful,
warm and icy powers. But Grampa Raincloud was
born with dark, evil powers of greys, blacks, and evil
storms which Granny couldn't control. He was planning
to steal all the animal and with granny out of the way
it was going to be easy.

Tom tried to send a messenger pigeon to the triplets
but Grampa cought it. He also cut the power line and
the telephone wires so there was a black out and no
phone calls, he even disabled all mobile phones somehow, Tom didn't know how he did it. The wind whistled
through the trees, the only noise to be heard in the
village. With no way to contact granny and Grandma,
dark shadows watching every thing and everyone,
what would they do? . . .

It's good that the sisters can sense Grampa
Raincloud or this story would never have had a happy
ending. When they sensed his evil they rushed back to
Tom and the village.

They were horrified as soon as they saw the
destruction and devastation when they saw what
Grampa was doing to the animals.

Soon they were face-to-face in a remarkable family
reunion (you could call it a family showdown).

One step closer, and Marmaduke get's it!" bellowed
Grampa, holding Marmaduke by his collar, dangling
him over a enormous vat of evilly black water.

"Oh no you don't!" cried Granny Rainbow, holding
up a vial, tightly stoppered, containing melted snow,
(the work of Grandma sunshine and Nanny Snow,

since there was no pure water to be found) sand—
from the magical beach—and a secret ingredient, which
Granny liked to call 'Goody-Goody-Two-Shoes' mix. "You
wouldn't dare, Gertrude!" sneered Grampa dropping
Marmaduke into the water.

"Tom!" screeched Nanny, with a croaky voice.

Tom was just in time to save Marmaduke from the
evilly black water, after rescuing all the other animals,
that is!

As Grampa was distracted by Tom, Granny threw
the vial at him and it smashed against him, drenching
him with extra-strong-Goody-Goody-Two-Shoes-mix (the
extra strong came from the magic sand).

Now, as the mixture hit Grampa everything was
restored, all the destruction gone as if it had never
came, all the animals saved and there was blackout
gone and the sun came out (maybe thanks to Grandma
Sunshine), but best of all, Grampa wasn't evil, and he
wasn't dark with his dark minions, he was now good
and bright and happy.

"Come in for cake and tea, everybody, even Grampa
Smiles." said Old Tom, waving his arm around,
"Everything is better now!"

"Of course!" they all chorused. So they all went into
Old Tom's house for cake and tea.

"How many sugars in your tea everybody, one or
two?"

"THREE!"

YOUR EDITING HEAD

When you are polishing your story, you are using a totally different part of your brain to the one that came up with all the ideas.

IDEA SIDE   EDITOR SIDE

Think of it as having a mini-me who sits on one shoulder, yelling 'Yay, great idea, go for it!', and another mini-me on the other shoulder who says 'that's not written very well. Stop. Go back and make it right.' (This mini-me is very similar to the Doubt Demon in some ways!)

It depends very much on the writer as to how they work with these parts of their brain. Some writers allow the editor-brain and the creator-brain to switch on and off very quickly, so they won't write much before they correct it, polish it, and move on. Others—like me—like to give their creator-brain free rein and get as much done as possible *before* they let their editor-brain in on the story because it interferes with how the story flows.

As you've discovered so many times already during this book, it's up to you to find out which method of working is best for you. And be careful that your editor-brain doesn't take over so much, it morphs into a Doubt Demon and stops you from writing anything because what you've written never seems perfect enough.

IN MY OPINION . . .

One of the things you can do to help polish up your stories—but only after you think you've done all you can on your own—is to find someone to read them and tell you what they think of them.

Now, right back at the start of this book, you might remember I mentioned that not everyone will love what you write. So you have to be prepared at this stage *not* to get a glowing report back from whoever you choose to ask. Remember that everyone is different in what they like to read, which is why there are so many different books in the world. People are allowed not to like your story for a variety of reasons. If they normally read adventure stories and you've written about ghosts, your story may not be (as we say in the UK) their 'cup of tea.'

Even so, if we find someone to read the story who will help us, whether they like the story or not, who is best to ask? And what do we do with what they tell us?

WHO TO ASK?

You can ask a parent/grandparent/best friend to read your story. They'll probably love it, because *you've* written it. However, they probably won't want to hurt your feelings by telling you anything they didn't like, so they won't necessarily be very useful in helping you to improve your story.

You could ask a trusted friend, someone who will tell you the truth without being mean. (It's a fine line!)

And of course, if you have a writing friend, someone whose stories you've read and liked, who you think writes well, you could always ask them . . .

Whoever you choose to ask, let them know what *you* want to know. Don't say 'Did you like it?' You're allowed to be specific. Instead, ask things like, can you find any spelling mistakes? Are my descriptions too long? Did you guess whodunnit? Do you think Gertie's a strong enough character? Is the climb up the mountain in chapter 7 too boring? I'm a bit worried the ending doesn't feel right . . .

Once you are feeling more confident in your own writing, you could even join an online writing community or a real live writing group and ask the people there. Most of the members will be writers too, and will have lots of thoughts to offer.

WHAT DO YOU DO WITH WHAT THEY TELL YOU?

Once your reader has read your story, there are three things you can do with any feedback they give you.

Accept it and act on it.

Amend (change) what you've written because the person feeding back has a point.

Reject it and leave things as they are.

Accept, Amend, Reject.

Accept

Some of the feedback *has* to be acted on. If your spelling is bad, or you are using punctuation incorrectly, you will need to put these things right.

No excuses.

Your reader might have spotted a formatting issue like an extra space, or two full stops at the end of a sentence. This may not happen so much if you are writing by hand, but you might have forgotten to start a new paragraph when you needed to, or missed off some speech marks. Again, this *has* to be altered, so you accept it. (As an aside, if you are handwriting your stories, try to make your writing reasonably neat. Otherwise your reader will spend precious time trying to work out what you've written before they can get stuck into the story!)

There may be a word missing, or another one repeated—these are things to sort out if you want your story to make sense.

Some of these sound like such tiny things to be worrying about—will a reader really spot the missing full stop at the end of the chapter? Yes. Yes, they will! And it can ruin the enjoyment of reading your story for them.

Amend

Sometimes you may decide to change your story because of what you've been told. The feedback might confirm something you're already feeling unsure about. For example, it could be that there's a weakness in the plot, or the way a character reacts to a situation doesn't feel real enough. If your feedbacker (I don't know if that's a real word, but I'm sticking with it) is picking up on the same thing that you're already wondering about, then it is probably worth looking at the issue and seeing if you can improve it.

Gut feeling is a wonderful thing—especially when you know in yourself that something's not working, (or if it's very good) and your reader confirms it.

It may be something much simpler than a problem with the plot—sometimes referred to as a plot hole—or an unrealistic character which needs to be amended though. Your reader might suggest you reword a sentence, and even gives you their version of it to make it easy for you! However, do you remember we talked about finding 'your voice'—that unique way of writing that only you can write? There is a risk that if you drop someone else's words into the story instead of using your own, your reader will spot them. (This actually happened to me, over one short sentence. It stood out a mile to the reader.) They won't necessarily think 'aha! different author', more 'I've been jolted out of the story because something doesn't feel right here'.

Whenever there's a suggestion of changing something *that you agree with,* try as far as you can to rewrite that sentence, paragraph, or chapter in your own unique way.

Reject

Should you always change everything that's been suggested by your reader?

No.

Why? Because this is your story, and sometimes, you need to stick to your guns. Let me give you an example.

READER 1

I don't like character X's name.
It doesn't sound manly enough.

> ## READER 2
>
> X is also the name of a well-known character in a famous film. Do you think you should change X's name?

Reader 1 is expressing an opinion. Reader 2 is pointing out a potential complication. If lots of people tend to think of the film character when they read the name X for the first time in my story, then I would consider changing the name thanks to Reader 2's feedback, but not based on Reader 1's.

Or how about this:

> ## READER
>
> I think it would have been much better if the butler had done it. I didn't believe for one minute it was the maid.

Now, if the whole point of your story is that the maid did it, whatever it was, and you don't want to change that fact, you don't have to. However, if the reader is also saying that they didn't believe that the maid was involved, you may now have to amend something in your story to convince your reader that she did, indeed, do it!

A Word about Writing Groups

In my experience, a writing club or group or community can be a wonderful thing to belong to. The members—all writers themselves—understand how hard it can be to write a story of any length, and if you are lucky enough to meet some experienced writers among them, they may well be generous with help and advice because at some point, they were exactly where you are now—and somebody helped them.

An ideal writing group should be able to:

- Encourage and boost your confidence.
- Offer constructive comments on how you can improve.
- Support you through difficult times (especially if you have decided you want to be published).
- Accept that not everyone writes for the same reason—you should be made as welcome whether you are writing for fun or because you'd like to be published one day.
- Give everyone a chance to share their work if they want to, but not force anyone who doesn't.

That said, there are some writing communities which operate very differently, and I would encourage you to try different groups if you are able to until you find one where you are comfortable.

And if you can't find a group, why not set one up yourself with some writing friends?

The End . . .

It's hard to know quite where to stop in a guide to writing stories! I've learned so much over the years, and am still learning, even now. I'm sure I could have told you so much more.

But I feel I've passed on here many of the things that've helped me, and as such, I've done as much as I can to help you in your own journey to write super stories and become a better writer.

I sincerely hope that although this is the end of this particular book, it's only the beginning of many more that *you* are going to write.

And one day, I may well be reading *your* story.

Acknowledgements

Thanks:

To Amanda D, Sarah H, and Aisleen H for letting me use their experiences with me as the basis for a lot of this advice.

To Mark B, who gave me the confidence to believe that what I know about writing and the advice I can give *is* worth sharing more widely.

To the team at Bedazzled Ink for letting me try my hand at nonfiction, for making this book such fun to read, and particularly to Casey, who made me realise in putting this guide together that I do a lot of things writing-related intuitively, and that I never really learned the facts which underpin it all.

And finally, to all the writers who've ever helped me, and to all the new ones who–I hope–will continue the great tradition of 'paying it forward'.

Katherine Hetzel is 'the short author who tells tall tales'. To date she has published two short story collections for younger readers, and five middle grade fantasy adventure novels with Dragonfeather Books. Her short stories have been longlisted twice and shortlisted once in the Leicester Writes Short Story Prize, and been published in around a dozen anthologies. *Cirque de la Vie* was a runner up in Retreat West's Quarterly Flash Competition March 2021. She blogs about life and writing at Squidge's Scribbles, runs a writing group called NIBS, and is a volunteer librarian at a primary school. She lives in the heart of the UK with Mr Squidge and has two grown up Squidgelings.